HEART WORK

HEART WORK

Poems by
Sharon Dolin

THE SHEEP MEADOW PRESS
RIVERDALE-ON-HUDSON • NEW YORK

All inquiries and permission requests should be addressed to: The Sheep Meadow Press, Post Office Box 1345, Riverdale-on-Hudson, New York 10471.

Photograph of Sharon Dolin by Star Black.

Designed and Typeset by the Sheep Meadow Press.
Distributed by the Sheep Meadow Press.

Printed on acid-free paper in the United States. This book meets the guidelines for permanence and durability of the Committee on Production Guidelines for Book Longevity of the Council on Library Resources.

Library of Congress Cataloging-in-Publication Data

Dolin, Sharon.
        Heart work : poems / by Sharon Dolin
            p.   cm.
        ISBN 1-878818-42-2
        I. Title.
    PS3554.O438H43   1995
    811'.54—dc20   95-39157
                                                        CIP

The Sheep Meadow Press gratefully acknowledges grants from the National Endowment for the Arts and the New York State Council on the Arts, which helped in the publication of this book.

For Barry

and in memory of my mother

ACKNOWLEDGMENTS

Grateful acknowledgment is made to the following journals, in which some of the poems, sometimes in earlier versions, first appeared:

Boulevard: "Reading," "The Bear"
Confrontation: "Heart Work"
Cornell Daily Sun: "Three Postage Stamps"
Oxford Magazine: "Human Table"
The Pennsylvania Review: "Family Rites"
Poetry: "If My Mother," "The Visit"
Poetry New York: "Portrait of a Clarinetist"
Salamander: "Salvation," "Tuscan Landscape with Self-Portrait," "Melancholia in Castiglione Messer Marino," "Piazza dei Cavalli Marini," "Out of Time," "Last Days"
The Threepenny Review: "Sketch of Paula Modersohn-Becker Dying After Childbirth"
Tikkun: "Loosening the Sealed"
The Times Monitor (Ithaca, NY): "Old Worlds"

"Persephone in Paradise" appeared in *The Book of Contemporary Myth* (Pittsfield: The Caitlin Press, 1988).

The following poems first appeared in the chapbook *Mind Lag* (San Francisco: Turtle Watch Press, 1982): "Sunday Meditation," "Trivento: A Provincial Diary," "Canzone of Dreams," "Letter from Salomé," "In a Market," "Pomegranates."

"Praying Mantis in Brooklyn" was awarded the 1990 Gordon Barber Memorial Award by the Poetry Society of America.

"Take Measure" was exhibited in "Heroism, A National Juried Visual Art and Poetry Exhibition," 1992, Peconic Gallery, Suffolk Community College, Riverhead, New York and appeared in the accompanying catalogue.

I'd like to thank Yaddo, the Virginia Center for the Creative Arts, and Palenville Interarts Colony for their generous support.

CONTENTS

Work of the eyes is done, now
go and do heart-work
on all the images imprisoned within you . . .

—*Rainer Maria Rilke*

I. PRAYING MANTIS

PARADISE

I.

I had thought it was there, in that still lake,
the unchangeable sameness of it—and we three women
plunging ourselves with pent-up relief
into the twilight heat. *It's an endless day!* I said,
close to the summer solstice.

I remember plunging on over my head and coolly wet,
looking back at you two: one dark, with beautifully
pendulous breasts, and one, Norwegian blonde with red skin
against the white places the sun had missed—slowly threading
into the thick green plush of water. Could this be anything
but paradise—with no fears, no hesitations anymore, after
an hour's ride in the car, lazy with sips of beer and heat?

It took hours for the sun to go down, or at least to lose
its reflected heat off the water. We lulled ourselves shore-
ward, until the caterpillars in hundreds, began their heavy
dropping from the trees: a bit less leafy after another day's
feeding—the steady pat-pat, like an afternoon shower.
And the frogs across the way waking up and sawing at each other.

II.

Then in New York, it's a breezy sun and a lazy
stroll along the esplanade, before the river,
where a young boy, crazy for a fish,
waits for his father's portable reel
to snare it up. *Oh, it's an eel, eel, eel; it's an eel.*
And running over I see

The father's hard shoe, stepping on the slithering footless
beast, to pry the hook from its muzzle. Still slithering,
the eel—like the dance of light on the river's coating—
shimmies its way toward the walk's edge, and blindly leaps
onto rock, and then leaps again.

The boy grabs it and the family quickly poses
before the camera: the boy heroic stands between
his parents, and between them is the eel.

PRAYING MANTIS IN BROOKLYN

Consider:
'(thoughts' torsion)'
                              —Louis Zukofsky

Before leaving for the house of prayer—
there—like a muezzin, crying the cat
looked out, shaking his tail, having seen
a praying mantis steady herself on the red brick
wall. Struck dumb, I watched him
watch a green blade fasten to the breeze four stories up.

The cat and I—ecstatic, frozen—gazed up
at a messiah of air—poised in prayer.
Vigilant—what could have brought her—inches from him
to such height—no bugs or insects—the cat
would eat her in a second—so still against the brick
she barely moved—did she sense us—inside the screen—we'd seen

Her turn her head toward us. As if having seen
us—as if to say: Keep looking up.
You think in Brooklyn nothing can move these bricks
but I've been sent—a prayer
to you—gravity can change—though the cat
would eat me—don't scold—without him

You would not have stopped—inside him
his hunger—you can say you've seen
an angel—green-bladed—cat
-walk your wall—always lift up
the head of possibilities—your poems—prayers
upon the Brooklyn air—can move these bricks

Mortar up your eyes—and these kids, bricks
in the street will blind you—neglect him
whose paws are a closed prayer
and you're lost—a woman on the ledge who's seen

a mantis fly—and you'll look down, lose what's up
there—gravity, unflinched, on a cat's

Back—strive to shadow this cat's
voracious play upon the screen—break bricks
the klezmer clap attack wakes up
even angels—the vicious way I bite the head off him
I've loved—biting the reasonable off what's seen
as useful—this too can be a prayer.

Fly, as I do, from bricks—unseen
on green wings—like this cat, scale prayers—
become weightless—angelic predator—Lift up!

"PRAYING MANTIS": EXTEMPORIZED

Fifty-six years later—the mantis still shocks—
an awareness of mystery in Brooklyn: the coincidence
of form inciting meaning—the poor returning to
soup kitchens, cardboard stalls. The subway still
a point of commingling.

The sestina arises from such visitations—
later drafts that might be adduced:
the mantis reappears, brown against the lip of
the gate as I rushed into the street—again toward
the house of prayer. Zukofsky—reverent but
non-sectarian—his mantis a prayer to save
the Depression poor—find a use-value as for paper
and stones.

As the mantis—a symbol
which eschews the symbolic. Still "the most pertinent
subject of our day—the poor," more repulsive than
this mantis, emissary of a peculiar beauty—whose colors
and presence are, thanks to a landlord who has
neglected the front yard all summer—as the sestina
crosses the boundaries between form and the formless
elastic—to a limit—obsessive as all passionate
thought must be.

> I think of the world's intransigence toward the poor
> toward workers
> toward the mystery that
> cannot be used as collateral

Someone spoke recently to me about "the quality of mind"
a woman lacked—What culture—Brooklyn least of all—
can bear to look up at what may bite the
Head off its quality of mind. The mantis, secure
in its death, forestalls the evaluative gaze.

Zukofsky—elevating Brooklyn's quality of mind
in the nineteen thirties—prophetic—flying in the face
of capital—as the mantis—ungainly—flew at his chest.

The questions asked then—who deserves to eat
who to have shelter
who to hurl garbage
that others may pick through humbly, of a Sunday evening
devoutly filling a sack—answered fifty years later.

In the house of prayer, at the Head of the Year,
a newborn father held up
his daughter so her eyes could receive the
impress of the scrolls, with their shining crowns
being danced through the aisles—a dream for the soul to
harbor—the Torah, ungainly in the woman's arms
—the mantis opening its wings.

Stones and bricks of light floating on the strength
of prayers—the rabbi exhorting us not to forget
the children—forty thousand—who would die
that day from an imposed fast, with no prayer
to sustain them—The mantis

A reminder of spindly form—the tenuousness of
who sleeps in a shelter—
When the garden is rudely
hacked—where will she go?

The bricks of Brooklyn—hard as the shell of an
insect—reminded, that a grasshopper
turned locust, changes its carapace
completely.

The mantis steadies herself on the gate's edge
having imagined her speech—
the sestina—a six-legged insect
preening through centuries

of "ungainliness" beating its wings
inside the hearts of Dante and Zukofsky.

The only form that can speak
with expanding wings—impassioned
intellection—the Head crowning
the Body.

READING

In the woods she has taken off
all but her chemise   she has
forgotten herself in her husband
is abandoned to reading
the moment inside her

momentary lover   as I am
abandoning myself to the voice
who shapes her story; it feels somehow
written only for me

though I sense someone
as I dip my head lower, who
wants to watch—as she was surely
watching her own self-

forgetting—someone beside me
on the train, perhaps, outside
the dream who confirms
the embrace—like the bedpost

when you shift between chapters
and are jostled and disturbed—someone
who wants to peer in and read
along, insisting, "This is not private,
you are not the only one."   As

Paolo, thinking himself alone with Francesca
   in her chamber, might have felt Dante's breath
   forming them into terza rima
interposing the line's breadth
   between the coupling pair;
   until the confirming death
of reader and shadowy husband's stare
   daggered them apart.

PORTRAIT OF A CLARINETIST

A cattle bell, *clarine*. You place
your fingers meant to rattle air upwards
from the Boehm stops—metal and ebony wood
—or is it *clair,* or Latin *clarus,* cork
edges greased into smooth oily turns
the pieces into a composite whole: clear.

So why, in the movies, when a long, winding
melancholic crawl of mood comes over in
clarinet, not clarion, but clear as the
heart's sobbing whisper—your sleep,
the clarinet-boy's silent whorl of breath
the reed from his tongue—does he, haunter
of my life, anger-steeped, now Pan-drowsing
by the bank of our urban bed, stir whatever's
deep: mud, the rushes, reeds of despair
then hope, then the high staccato quiver
of tongue on reed on bank on bed.

LOOSENING THE SEALED

The words have already been written in
our hearts intertwined—and whether you
will advance in your clarinet and whether

I will continue to hunt up the right words
in the right order as though my life depended
on it.

And it does, as does yours on how smoothly staccato
goes—and if you don't find the proper reed, where
will the music go—suffering in squeaks

And if I don't rediscover the word for being:
meaning a sentient existence, blooded
by happenstance . . .

In this day, all will be sealed: who shall
live and who shall only appear to

Who shall carry their spirit around like
a long bothersome tail—vestigial, and meaningless
saved only by a stroke of history

And with each step, the small bones—brittle
from lack of use, crack beneath the shoe's hard shell.

Sometimes, I think the clarinet is your
ebony tail—that you have drawn to you and
refashioned for song—so long

Useless, bored now
with stops and metal taps, each note
sounds blue until you take it up

Rework the scale so the spirit, so long
trapped within, effluviates

Beckons in the direction of the
word I still seek.

SUNDAY MEDITATION

Today, in my sun lethargy,
I crouch, reading in a well,
in my grassy yard at the bottom-most part
of this windowed ring of houses.
Here by the Buddha and potted jade—
so full of sun its thick fleshy tips
have reddened:

I do what many Sunday dreamers do:
thinking in this warm breeze that stirs me
about a certain man who has brightness still
to stir me with a different warmth.
So that to look at the leaves of this plant
or to watch a bumblebee wholly
swallowed—in its swallowing—up by an orange
buttercup: is to know there are many gardens
I can sit in, that the one I lost last fall
was the loss of hope.

And what if I have done no gardening this summer?
When the sprinkler runs, the snails
cover the plot and are feasting.
I was so horrified, the one time
when several crawled up the retiring Buddha's
cement-draped shoulder, covered the
suggestion of an earring; and when I wanted
to suddenly kill all the snails, a friend calmly said,
What right have you to choose lives?
And when I answered, *But they eat up whole gardens,*
she shook her head the way Albert Schweitzer shook
mosquitoes out of his hair.

So perhaps I have a garden of snails
and bricks and a tangle of fuchsia-rose trees
under whose blooms the Buddha—and some transitory cats—sit
and only I am the removable plant—taking

the morning sun and listening to the clatter of plates
and children, a Schubert sonata, the running, barking
down-the-steps dog, the clattering wind-sticks.

And when, sitting in this garden,
I think of this particular man—
a different understanding
of sinning and love grows in me:
that to not use the garden we are in—
and for this man to not find what he can do
in the world (as the snails to their watery crawl)—
is the only sin; that the lettuces and carrot seed
I might have tossed are gone, while here,
surely I am the gardener of some things
and perhaps of this man—who wants planting—
and I will not say flowering:
for the root of the carrot is very sweet.

NIGHTMARES

Last night you turned
again—hovered above
like I was the ground that gave you meaning,
but even then you had another love
and could not stay.

When you turned
into a woman—haughty
in the sun of an Italian terrazza
(and I loved you still) your face
told me I wasn't the only one
and looked out to the sea.

On waking,
I saw you wore your uniform
to bed—armored with drink and
sweat and clothes to bandage
up any new wound I might give.

A Delilah I had to become—unwrap
you—fingers impressing

                      swoons

          all the tenderest places . . .

shielded
       even when bare.

ST. JUDE

Even at our most intimate
there is a saint encircling your neck
dangling over me
or tangled in your hair.

Sometimes I think he is to protect
you from me

and when I think of you, in that
old country, I can be sure of one thing:
that same figure will interpose
itself between you and her
in argument, in lovemaking.

At least you are never
completely uncovered.

But how I wish the thought
of my arms around your neck—
like a talisman of memory—
could protect you.

Oh guardian of impossible causes
what keeps him from me—

what figure do I wear
daughter of an older religion—
one of the stiff-necked ones
whose king could kill for a
new bride

and yet his psalms
are the ones we both share.

Perhaps the voice of David
curls itself around

my neck, intertwined with the fine
hairs at the nape—

David singing at midnight
abundant praises for
the chief musician

and I am of the people
of impossible causes
still praying for a return.

HUMAN TABLE

for Primo Levi

1.
Turning the elements into elemental resemblances:
Argon, the inert response of your ancestors
to change; your friend of Iron clawing
his way up a cliff-face.

As you are called Levi, servant
of priests, mediating between the desirous
and the wise

now tell me, if every Jew were
partisan, what element would that have been

if every fascist, Uranium, burning up
their own fingers, what quick half-lives
they'd have had, how long-lived you
and your compatriots.

Instead you chose to be the undiscoverable
one   out there in the woods ringing
every town, in caves, under the earth of cities—
the reactant: stable, changing
the combinations of the known world.

2.
                         Amid tree rustle,
shuffle of trains: the roar of the moment
suffices. You understood, Primo,
the sinuous heated shapes of glass tubes, the reactive
quality of the elements   stable, even in a fascist mine
or a Nazi lab
                         belying the human laws that

tend toward irrational density: a lazy lab girl
tendering the hands of a lieutenant, a vengeful
son finding some sample of race to call dog. Truly, you
found no *common good,* no community of workable elements
in combination.

                                          Only locales of the ostracized,
the overmilked. Mad chemists striving for the elemental
purity amid the clotted knot of being.

3.
Wading through molecules of memory
I expect to find a path
through the chemist's door: he'll be there
scribbling
in the half-light the glass tubes transluce

turning down the palms of his hands, gliding
his eyes up an arm to where the finer hairs grow
atom–perfect, forming his thoughts.

JACOB AFTER FORDING THE JABBOK

All night long I
wrestled with an angel—his face
obscured by hair the color
of light—arms, strong thin
swords   we tumbled
on the road as two animals
in the heat of spring—we could not be
parted—bless me, I said—and he touched
my thigh—the hollow of my thigh
and my desires were parted: the upper
from the lower—as in my dream
of angels going up and coming down—
I strove to master desire with
force and I was mastered
by his blessing—as a woman
by the strength of her loving foe—
as a man by the hollow
that divides him from himself.

FAMILY RITES

I know you are not in town
by the way the snow falls, transparent
on the walks—and the yellow leaves below
the house, canopy the windows against the grey.
I stay inside all day—arrange the hours into
a hapless crossword of meals and phrases—
Leopold Bloom leaving a restaurant with too much
scupping of meaty juices, enters a pub for wine
and cheese sandwich.

Evenings I drown before a large screen:
the French peasants almost speaking Italian,
the grand-mère smirks as she shakes hot
coals from her clogs, then slips them on.
The dough so huge it takes a man's
rough shouldering to knead his weight into
the vat; when he dies, his eldest son must
cut the bread.

I tell you these things to remind myself
you are not here—are eating dinner with what
will always be your family—they pass the polenta
before you—your stomach gets filled—you cut
the bread and hand your father the *doutz*—that crusty
end of sweetness: it's his right, you think, as he takes
it, while you're remembering the day before: when,
father before doctor, he probed your knee
for the place where the stiffness sets,
and you told him—yes—there's the pain.

AGAINST ANGELS

I once was touched by an angel—
blessed and healed, shuddered
around, caressed even kissed

until he crumbled
at the pages of
the earth or the
sound of dissonant words.

His wings got tangled
in my hair—his beard
made of fire scorched
my neck.   Not knowing
Hebrew well enough, I barely
spoke to him—and wrote inside
of books.

In love with the bodies of words
I failed him   in love with
transparencies of song   he fled.

TRIVENTO: A PROVINCIAL DIARY

1.
So you too leave—
when my pink scarf silences
me into sleep

I awaken and you've gone swimming
we will never touch
beneath
so many cigarettes

There is an illness
which makes me climb steps while
a full moon burns your temples.

In this mountain village I am
growing a family—a sixth finger that
the gypsies will cut while I'm
sleeping and hide in their bread

Under breaths of black cloth
while a cat turns in its sleep

This is a new spell—where the
sun burns in shadows and
I talk to you only in sleep.

2.
Here in this village
every night is a full moon
and someone to walk me down
stone steps fixed in place

This village is older than Roma, someone says
even the cats go back to a different
time as do the mountains—rock hard
and dry

When every night is moonlight
and a sister has worn black for three years
I forget purple has a place
in this world

Forget to stop eating
scamorsa, dolce, pasta—rolled and cut
two hours before on a marble-top.

Sleeping all morning—the *temporale*
hitting the window but I dream
on—the glass unbroken.

CANZONE OF DREAMS

1.
You, oh do you understand the distance
that loves to separate would-be lovers
that diaphanous gauze, Fantasy, under which
the torso grows faint, and then clearer?

We are not even sending letters.
Over the telephone we exchange dreams:
a noonday one you had of the kindest woman
who defrosts your freezer and you are loving her for it.

Then I wire back: a giant woman orders me
to clean the perfectly dry, white bathtub
(the same one you are about to step into?);
we ponder your longing for warmth, my fear
of no water.

Today when we talked of typewriters
I felt us the prisoners of our timetables:
locked into bus rides, I started dreaming us
both in your afternoon bath, the typewriter
pulled in with us even all the sticky bus rides
I tell myself to keep taking—somehow begin
bulging with water.

2.
Now I am thinking of Dante's song-poems:
canzoni to a gentle, yet stony, lady;
always he ended them with a *congedo:*
that tail of stanza in which the poem
turned dove, becomes both the beloved
and its messenger—and shows, finally, its own
desperate feathers.

Who else can I tell of yesterday's enticement:
lusinghiero—the allure of a single word—

and in the saying, I am taken, taken
in by a moral man whose name means *evil head*—
Malatesta—even though he carried more limpid ideals
more *lusinghieri* than we can ever speak of.
And I, being lover and *allured—lusinghiera*
ripple my tongue over it, over this hot coffee
in the bright sun.

Or to say when I speak to you, and you ride
your cab all night . . . that too, is a kind of dream,
like letting people into your bath;
and I start to wonder if you finally enter
my *stanza* and we open our shirts,
for a while will we both awaken?

Go, you dream-song of prisoners, of letter-writers
of phone-callers. Go, find the one I am loving
in this parched song. Find the one with rain
and a metered car, and tell him, before the desert
wind comes and he leaves—
I am waiting: my mouth—the smallest of wells—to be filled.

THE THIRST FOR MORE

Francavilla al Mare

Green leaves of the basil plant, the pungence
of fresh lavender at the door.
Here, Rose of Sharon flourishes everywhere
called hibiscus by Chiara, the consummate gardener,
who tends even the afternoon haze which hangs over Francavilla
so that the sea we languish for
is more the remembered pearl
than the foam.

This morning the sea was an ocean and the boy
had to whistle me out
before I could even approach
the currents that would
not have let me turn back.

The other day, while traveling down the ripe belly
of Umbria with its umbilical of sunflowers
and olives, I had to go toward the train whistle
though I longed for the Ligurian aquamarine waters
where fish were brushed in schools, as though by invisible
curtains, among the rocks and coral.

To embrace this other sea while my heart also clenched
for Siena with its mad traffic of songs of the *Contrade,*
in every corner a scarf or banner waving: even in
the courtyard of Saint Catherine, where
the horse of the Goose was led in a fanfare
of offerings and prayers,
a harp loosened the fibers of morning one by one
so that I thought, for a moment, I'd entered
a terrestrial paradise.

But time, the strongest undertow
has dragged me farther and farther from
the crush of pleasure by the shore.

I leap into the future, I drown
in the mundane
nap of coffees.

At four in the afternoon, the dizzy
traffic of shops pulling up their Venetian blinds,
the small agonies of the beach:

Whether to plunge into the unforgiving sea
or buy diaphanous flowers woven into a scarf
of hunger by the Senegalese vendors.

The wisest course (this, I didn't know):
always leave something undone, unyielded to, untasted
so that your soul remains unquenched of
every thirst or—better still—drink heavily
of the sea to bring on a heartier thirst.

SKETCH OF PAULA MODERSOHN-BECKER
DYING AFTER CHILDBIRTH

So easy to pry into the
symbolic: the knife in its
reflective pane
of cutting timbre—glancing off
skins of peaches
apples dropped to a still
fuzzy readiness . . . all the life
in the room slowing
backed into this
corner and tilted up: a coral-blue
sea panel penetrates
a midnight drinking glass.

Oh mother, you should never have
left Paris, yourself remained
a child painting
the knife stuck in the band of light
fern fronds lying
all along the table . . .
instead of turning back to him
your Orpheus, so
in the middle
of the night you'd hear my cry: go
down to retrieve me—lose
yourself in sea caverns.

II. HEART WORK

HEART WORK

Having reached the clandestine park
where all the birds unpearl their feathery necks,
having absorbed the last images of her: porcelain
head unsteady on spindly frame, then
swollen and dying

Now do heart work:
Take down the angry pose—the nervous
lip-biting, pacing inside the small room of want—
to find a self pinched back
imprisoned still by images
not fully risen to the surface.

In the photographer's studio, so much is soaking
in the hearty red fluid light
I'm having trouble getting back into the room
without tears to turn the handle,
pull the darks out of the lights
and greys: to look her image back
into its separate gloss, not glaze
over and become its mirror.

The work of separate selves continues: mine beneath
fan-blades that flick the breeze like lines
of verse to cool the heart; hers beneath
the earth, outside of time to mark its
boundaries, the silence that encases
all these calls.

IF MY MOTHER

were not an emaciated bird
who stands shorn of everything
but her pocketbook
she dangles—empty
save for her lipstick and pounds of change—
the sac worn outside
like the one in which I curled, slept, sucked
my thumb—if there weren't so little left of her
barely keeping herself erect—how could she
ever keep anyone—herself—warm again—

if my mother were not a flamingo that we leave in
the hospital lobby—half-terrified
that her bed—so close to the other patients'
coats—might threaten her—my mother,
who has fought her visions for 45 years
and received no medal—
watched her husband wrench away out of disgust
and grief—if her newest children were not wires
she sees everywhere—sparks
of her life escaping to endanger her . . .

then I could not be brave—
become like
my sister—unshaken who holds me in
the bathroom of some forsaken diner
in New Jersey—after my mother has
cursed the meal, everything, even the rice pudding: *slop,*
real slop—and we have to laugh
at how right she is—
as she gets up
and hobbles out of the diner
to the parking lot—
not knowing where we are taking her
wounded by all the people who
might kill her

except for me and my sister
who glide her
to the hospital emergency
just let me put on my lipstick
refusing my compact mirror—an expert
against a parked car's reflecting glass—she
takes up the pink stick and traces—her better
lips—the ones she will purse and hold and
question me with
when she goes to sign herself in—
waiting for me to nod, *yes, it's okay, you can sign*
no one will keep you here forever—no one will
shock you again—no wires—no one
will do that to you again.

THE VISIT

There will always be this place
inside
where I feel her absence
where I feel the echo of her lost voice—
the one she would have used to call me
back from sadness   as she had to be
called so many times   back from madness.

What would it take to summon her—
Not having an address, just a marker
for where she is not

I can only go and visit
her absence   her remains
which become less and less like her
more and more like the earth and trees,
the sky she continually faces.

I'd rather picture her under the sea
hair waving to the fishes and the brine,
being washed clean by
sharks and plankton

than under those pines by
the stone bench: one more desiccating root
in a garden of bones.

NOT QUITE PARING HER FINGERNAILS

She entered the curtains and
worked the switches and gears
I thought she was Oz—
great! powerful! magnificent!—

my voting Mom.
I'd sit outside and look at the faces
on the littered pamphlets
knowing which one she was
conjuring
in her booth of power.

As now, descending into
the basement lunchroom
of the Brooklyn public school,
taller than usual amid the
children at low benches eating
the sandwiches of my youth,
I enter behind the pulled curtain,
bereft of her, finally, and
scan the names. Like
the unmoved mover, or my mother,
judge with the flick of a lever
and seal it with a firm yank
of the flat metal pole
that sends me back out into the world.

WHERE

When I lifted him
for the last time,
all that hot angry possessive fur,
talons ready to strike
any rival—even me—
to keep me—
and lowered him into
a box
where the vet
syringed him unconscious
before the liquid stroke and the burning flame
singed all fur

Where do they go—

Is it like in my dream
of Dante, turned stray
and caught on the mezzanine, that
in between
floor
unreachable?

And she—where—she who bore me—
for the second winter, covered with a thin sheet
—in a rich mahogany box (or is it pine?)
when the earth hardens and freezes—tell myself
she is not there
amidst the trees—not left out
to the elements,
having become elemental
but where—not on the phone,
the forgotten message that stirs the day
into a distant murmur of some other conversation
—but the lost voice.

Where—they—having never met—too feeble
she—to climb the many steps
to where
he'd haunt the stairs—guardian
gone mad—as had she—
the two who loved me most
(human and animal)
conversant now in some other tongue.

The question dropped from the books,
the great wisdom, unspoken,
from which we sprang:
Where have you gone?
as even God asked once
of Adam before there was death or loss.

THE BEAR

The bear was there
he was going to help me eat
some meat
but when he'd burrowed his snout
and sniffed me out—
my crotch, my arm—
and held my skin between his teeth,
I thought,
better send him away
and cried out.

Then, at the cemetery party
an ordinary family gathering
I was kneeling over the graves near the headstones
with my sister
my grandmother raving with slashed
earlobes her face deep red
until the mask got torn
away—shredded off into my mother's face
composed and calm: there she was
and I held her hand—held her
soft hand and thought how I'd been missing her
so this was where she'd gone
'life . . . death' I thought to tell
her how all we know is this,
but said nothing, assuming she already knew
and just held on
gazing into the serenity
she'd become.

SALVATION

*Man's salvation is whatever has, as he has, a beginning and an end,
whatever can start over. . . . When there is nothing left, there will
still be sand. There will still be the desert to conjugate the nothing.*

—*Edmond Jabès*

1.
Start again without—
this kindling over
this getting through
this filling up
this triumph over the lack.

The Sinai haunts me with its fullness
only there: to receive the word in the wild
only with eggs in my basket, *t'marim* and pita
the Bedouin girls, giggling,
wake me with each morning
before the ascent.

I have wanted you against the mad wall
but she intervened.
You blocked the snowstorms and
the sand and if only I could have seized
you—then—when her face was
a blowfish, red, lifted from the water
and we wanted to let it back
down into the sea, but she said
*No, turn the television this way before
I'm too weak and get me a soda,
this ice cream is the only thing
I can still eat*

because the hook of this illness
has stuck her in the roof
of her mouth

If March winds are still possible
              blow me into that realm:
                    of sand and hunger.

But I have to go back to the desert, to a place
where water is the forbidden fruit
and what you perish by are stones caught
in the camel's pads—or your own mistaking
of the sun for the grin on the side
of God. You, too, immeasurable
fecundity by the waters, move inland.

     To find that what might
     have saved her was to have fed her
     back to her own madness
     until she exploded
     into health

          with sand in her last breaths
          she entered the wind.

2.
That thing happened to her—
that small quiet greatness of knowing
this is the last conversation
this my name, this I love you

these the pads of her fingers still soft
still gripping mine

looking from one slit eye—
(as a great sage, lazy
lizard, cornet of resistance,
old sea captain, paranoid
doorkeeper)—

then this disappeared.

3.
The first time you realize—that time
when you realize it—as it's happening
that it will continue to happen
and be marked
that late bright October Sunday
mounting the winding strip to the hospital
that Sunday, sunny and warm when the motorists feel free
and unencumbered

already foretold, that I would remember that
day's unfolding:
the Halloween skull laughing
above the silverware tray
in the cafeteria

keep returning to and playing
that *it* back over and over

the queasy stomach, the cafeteria visit
to down Coca-Cola, then tea
then the climb
          upstairs
                    into inevitability

because that's what we're talking about
because that's what remains.

4.
About this mourning, it is mostly
nothing different: just strange pock
marks of absence—like the blood spots on her skin—
the telephone not ringing, my message machine not
picking up her blowsy Brooklyn voice filled
with pain and childbirth, filled with eating and hunger
filled with motherlust and hatred
filled with the clicking needles of inquisitiveness, how

could her daughters thrive, how could she be left
to mildew in a house, watch the dust and cockroaches
take over, her mother lose threads in the soup and she herself
drop fifty pounds so that she felt
like a refugee from a private war

raising her nightgown once to show me.

5.
Dear Mom,
Now that you're gone
I can tell you what I've never
been able to say: like Persephone I hated the spring
returning to you, to the soil of grains
and young birds—though the summer
sea consoled me. Being near you
decimated me. So I let him take me
on his chariot of flesh—the flowers were
just a ruse—his briny belly drew me
and I clung to him like oxygen
his difference the only relief.
Mother, I never needed mirrors more
than when you were around,
to fall away into anything
blissful, somnolent.
When you took your watery eyes with you
I could climb out again—
whole—and pace the earth
not owing any say-so to you.

6.
There
she was beautiful, intact
where I had come out of—almost five
years after my sister
the only place left that was whole
a moss brown, lighter than mine
quiet among the body's heaving

and turning back into soil—a color as light
as sand, but darker than the desert.
That's what remains a long time under the earth—that tunnel
through which we slid—and her fur
promising protection, as did her mouton coat
under which I hid
wrapping myself around those trees in stockings.

7.
The day after my first visit—
the tubes already dripping into her arm—
she wheeled herself over
to look at photographs of Italy, eat
chocolates out of ravenous grief
as though she already knew.

That night I argued with customs:
I am who I am—not
the old lady found dead in her airplane seat.
Someone had switched the passports
and now I had hers, but couldn't he see:
I was me, not her—never her—that mirror shattered.

8.
The assaults of the heart
on the body are many,
he said, when I shrieked
as he ate a lipstick, then
some red rouge powder—the kind
she was so good at wearing.

9.
The silence
all around
that first time when the flame
licked over us and we came and
came in the grieving light. Her light,
warm and yellow and still redolent

of her in this world.
If I tell you I am sick with grief
and want cleansing will you hold me
if I tell you and tell you
that you are captious, cold, then
hot, I'm pushing against some
outer wall but the buses are taking you
out of here.

Wanting, wanting, a polecat on the fence,
some days are unfocused, dark gravy
others are red searing light that burns
clear through.

Have a changing vision,
it will hurt you either way.

10.
Though she couldn't read Hebrew,
now she visits me at synagogue
where the prayers all finally make sense

once out of her body
my mother has united all truths:

tears, Hindu burnings
the swaying Kaddish in my study
the lovers' swivel, Urdu poetry

as the flame burned down
in the glass globe, her soul rose further up

I know each time I step
out of the shower she peruses
my body—her chief pleasure being beauty—

and that the nights you pull me closer
she smiles above us,
finally able to mount the forty-seven steps to watch

circling through the spheres, my horizon
of grief and joy, vanishing
behind her lids, filtering into the air I breathe

whenever I hold things
or put lipstick on, or eat
chocolates,

it's for her smile, for that opening
in my head.

III. LOST LETTERS

PERSEPHONE IN PARADISE

When I return for a visit
Eve is temperamental, yells at her husband
for not washing the car. In the yard
apricots are ripening—falling
into my touch from untended branches.
She says they're too pulpy for her.
When I bite into one—a small pocket
of juice around the pit: this is paradise.

The mountains she calls hills rise
up like Elysium from the beach
the ocean—cold—but bluer than her irises
I dive into the slap of wave on wave—
memory lapped onto this present scene
while her husband, drunk on sunshine, hides
his face in the sand.

In Paradise everyone has marital difficulties
can't cut perfect avocado halves into each
other's salads. With so much spilled light
their skin darkens, closes up.

Perhaps the Creator made a mistake letting them
back in on a permanent basis.

Better to live in darkness for half a year
with a husband who traffics in the endings
of things—and after, rise sated from hibernation
a tourist in light who blinks at such brightness

Than to go blind with incessance—lose
the taste for fruit plentifully
dropping beside your lover onto the field's floor.

THEATER OF MEMORY

If place embodies
spirit in the world

how count on bliss

when the route is so singular
the apple we ate

brought forgetting into the world
and precisions of memory

to say nothing of
a hillside near the Pacific

where the small grape vines you planted
already cluster into

your dream of wine
the horses shake themselves

free of wind and desire
but you and I—steeped

in casual glances

what do we shake off, what do we
put on?

THREE POSTAGE STAMPS

DEUTSCHE BUNDESPOST across the top.
An odd drawing. Even wearing a dress, her torso seems bony.
Sitting at a writing table with a blank book
caught (or pausing) to look up. Her drawn face
in a thin smile revealing small spaces between her teeth,
the ridged bangs of her hair clipped so short
they seem an ill-fitted wig, her signature
scrawled in red across her book her watch-banded arm:
(ANNE FRANK-12.6.1929-31.3.1945) across the bottom.

nederland sideways, then simply *ANNE FRANK*.
A close-up. Plump cheeks in a girlish grin, her wavy front-hair
pulled to one side with a barrette.
Here, Anne's young face—younger than the German one—
is the way her father, Otto, probably remembered her.
I'm certain it must have been her father
who took the photo of her almost giggling,
the trace of a dimple in her chin.
And how it must have lain in his memory:
a still in a father's mind of his youngest girl's face
beaming out at him with no sense of pain
before the hiding.

And I can imagine young girls everywhere
who grow up reading her diary and soon start their own,
who, loving their fathers and feeling, late at night,
their bodies developing in that painless, maddening way,
are less scared for it, imagining what could be:
days of total silence, nights when the family must stir
like cats, prowling in each other's hair.
Here, Anne is looking at nobody. There are no lights.
She is up in the attic with Peter
or she is alone with her words.

THE HOUSE OF LOST LETTERS

     In Bogotá
if there is such a house, as Márquez says,
where an old man stoops
deciphering someone's wishes without
an exact address: "To the woman who goes
to La Iglesia de las Armas every
Wednesday at five," "To the man who smiled before the tram
carried away his face last Tuesday afternoon,"
then surely there must be others.

Perhaps even in Brooklyn,
in the post office where, as a child,
I was fascinated by the small rectangular
stories I discovered there every Saturday.

As my father's shoe kicked
forward a stack of brown boxes
I'd read of a man *WANTED*
for mail fraud—and murder—
Considered Very Dangerous
usually armed, a tattooed heart on his left
breast, a birthmark on the back of his neck.
Then I'd study the photograph—full face, profile,
any body part with unusual markings—
expecting to see, when I turned around, the man
or woman—usually a killer—waiting
in the Stamps Only line—or, now when I think of them,
at the solitary door, ringing to retrieve
a lost letter.

OLD WORLDS

When your hand refills the glass, the perfume of Belgium
memories the air; then you tell me there is nothing
in Ithaca, a dead town of bridges built over ravines;
above walk scholars mincing words with all
they have not lived. We can go for a drive—there,
you say, it becomes real again—the small town that is
not looking up its own sleeve. I can almost go with you.

We have destroyed the night—sleep in the active sounding
of each other's bodies; your room stays dark; we miss
the sun rise, but could live life out this way—the soft
plane of your back trying not to wake, your eyes
sheathed under, shying off the stranded light of day.

Tell me of those moments, when kept captive by
a mother and daughter buying St. Nicholas cakes,
your soul burst itself with desire, not for them,
but for its own dream of itself which these two
refracted back.

But that was Belgium, where a twelfth century church
was your personal landmark, and the pain of who you were
could catch onto the motorcycles or the torn corners
of light collecting in canals.

And what is different about that city and this
Ithaca I could make mythical by a five years return?
Here, in America, those moments I call a waking up
never happen, not even when I am beside you
thrusting myself in touch so that the shape and limit
of who we are has changed, not even then can I wake you
to that desire, that boundless reach and stasis.

I think now Ulysses never left home—waged a war
against his own desire; turned over in bed and there she was
by the window, weaving his dream of return into and out
of the fibers of her hair.

IMPERFECT

As this boardwalk in early spring
nicks in the two
by fours that trip me running
skeletons of the past—the stark Wonder
Wheel, frozen and the Steeplechase
one old man—shirtless, grey-
chested, wanting a winter tan

so are you beautiful

the thin tracery where your nose
once was torn from place
your knuckle's almost severed
tendon—larger—that holds
a bulky ring
and the tender spot in your upper chest
where a fencing blade pierced through

all the wounds that have made
a history of your body

as the history of this waterfront
is beautiful: hurricane-made cliffs
from these rocks twenty-five years ago,
so that to say *esplanade* was to name
this broken-up wildness   separate
from the crescent beach

where to swim meant climbing
down to meet the ocean
at a raw slap
where crabs nipped
and to stay above
where even sidewalk—too buckled
to risk a baby carriage—
was how we learned to walk the border.

TRAIN TICKET IMPROV

Providence will be blue
Boston will be red—
when you get up take your
ticket with you, then put it
back right where I put it.

Providence will be blue—when you
meet me at the station, put
your lips up to my ticket
then press them—right back red—
Boston.

When your lips get up blue
to my red and you put them—
Boston—up my back—where you
put them—take me—right there.

Boston will be red—get
your ticket ready—when I land
you get up—lift mine
when you go and put yourself
—right back blue.

Where I put you it will be
red—take yourself, get up
Providence will be where
I put you—blue ticket, press
up, get Boston, get in
yours.

LETTER FROM SALOMÉ

Here is a love which is so wicked it defies
both its partners:
slices chunks off cat tails
strings cow eyes blind
around a neck.

Six thousand miles separate the way our legs cross
six thousand miles

of drums tapping at a cheek
cowskin and livers shimmering in alleyways.

There are surely several beers
separating us
several nights
when fingers became
what they touched

dark streets turned to flatbread
and more and more faces
more faces—hit faces
than shoes to be shined
and dead fish stinking
up—

I'm trying to come home to you
on the strings of this English no one speaks
this desert keeps me on the bus
water so salty it burns
worse than sand

and I must breathe through scarves
dance with coins falling through
my hair.

IN A MARKET

In a market
you are bargaining to return to me
while Arabs speaking the language
of sand on the tongue
sell postcards of themselves
riding camels covered with
mirrors and pink satin.

Your blonde hair could fetch twenty gelibas
in this desert market
and a kiss from a woman's mouth
smelling of sweet sesame bread.

When you return we bargain
for each other's hands
shaking off smiles with
sandy sleeves,
the feel of camel ribs playing
over your eyes
when you touch me.

PHYSICS OF MEMORY

On 14th Street, as I wait for coffee, the heat
pouring onto my legs
from the bottom of a freezer-case,
I remember you describing that time in Calcutta
you awed the examiners with logic:
Though you'd never seen a refrigerator, you knew
it had to pour out heat. So they brought you
to the States, but what comes over

Must release itself. So for the heat in your lungs
you grasped beer after beer, coffees midday
over the chessboard. Never so much a Hindoo
as in New York; what compresses cold, pours
out warm. In winter one year you disappeared:
the heat—one night between us—frozen.

SPANISH SNAPSHOTS

Beneath the looming cut-out wall—
it's as though all men
and boys were taking their daily exercise
below the prison's multiple black eyes.

A woman breathes under a market
table, a man's head noosed
inside the drapery reads a newspaper.

In the Spanish man I loved: so much sadness
in the cast in one eye I thought,
then, when I held him, I held
Franco's madness.

Is that why I return to these bruised images—
the whores of Mexico with lips
like jutting horns

the boy being beaten each night
then locked in a room, his father bringing
women back from the clubs to where he lay
curled inside a whorled horn.

It took years to learn compassion
entraps the gazer with the gazed—so that the snapshot
his mother gave me

of the gap-toothed boy
by the fountain before she fled
was what I held up to read
his cruelty by—believing he could choose

how deeply the blows would go.

THE DOMESTIC FASCIST

Anger still rises against you
for the time my father

waited, good-humored, downstairs
denied entry

he came, bearing gifts, oblivious
to the engines of hatred churning
above.

Witless I ran up and down—like
messengers passing between ghetto
and death chaperones and compromising
everything.

You would not listen   I brought up
a photo of your mother to intercede
but you were on the bed, paralyzed

by your anger, by your lies, by
the guilt over the Jewish women whose
hairs you had parted.

Nothing breeds hatred like intimacy. You
demanded I soothe you, rub your temples.

When you broke the windows of our house
I had to live within jagged spires

praying you would turn human again. That
was the fatal mistake: when kindness goes
it can never be imported.   So you loved

music, teared your face over quartets
of Jewish musicians
while I blundered through the house
of your rage, begging for

a reprieve
and a kiss to call me human.

COLORBLIND PAINTER

My brown dog is dark grey.
Tomato juice is black. Color TV
is a hodge-podge. My paintings
once shaped of carnival glass
have been syringed of color.

So I've taken to painting the room I see:
grey walls, chairs of granite, a table
of lead on which lie grey speckled
bananas made of mealy stone, oranges
shorn of their name encased in black
skins. Sometimes I close my eyes in
order to eat, or the grapes I pierce
squirt black juice, and sodden plums
acquire the vertiginous feel of fossils
softening up with life.

Now I roam the streets of night-towns
enter a night world where
diners glow in the raw steak of
3 a.m.
when the waitress approaches her face
wavers up from the underworld
serves me eggs—the yolks I know
partake of that dark socket among the trees
and coffee is the sweet, liquid slate
I down before the day explodes
its bomb in the terrible crater of the east.

TAKE MEASURE

*. . . Who shall measure the heat and violence of the poet's heart
when caught and tangled in a woman's body?*
                                                    —*Virginia Woolf*

Her heart, not so hot as to singe—the lancet
through the unhinged door
finds no wound. She is a healed thing, hovering
behind a newspaper, tangling—measurably.
If the sound suits her she gets carried
to the man on the subway   in the next room
as she undresses; this chair is felicitous.
Now she has two rooms—her own bathroom
triggering her eye
not merely an adjoining study to the sex parlor.

Steadying the horse above the prismatic glass blocks,
she has her own tiger, her own millinery industry, a surge
in the closet toward the well-wrapped basket of ardor.

The circus woman with geometric breasts and tough calves
this modern New York woman poet—as anomalous as
unnamed petals, phloxes of unwilled arrogance,
unlike her four-hundred-year-old sister
hawks her poems in the small press or, rather, is hawked
by weather reports and cactus flowers, cuff links
to be read. Ropes around the brass horse,
at a demonstrated vigil for the shushing of a male
novelist, but at herself?

Tangled in a woman's body: drafts of poetic prose
as though unable to separate
the washing properly (her study is overrun with clay
flutes, totem cats): the white socks from the blues
and reds, the poems from the greeting cards—
to take the stairs by twos and not be seen
again until the news—she sends the greetings,
she is a perfect holiday.

POMEGRANATES

To eat a whole one at one sitting
is to descend forever into the winter

                              willingly.

Calling them Chinese Apples
              though they're still from Israel

where I watch a young boy stop
every few minutes in his own sweat
to reach and pluck

                              a red globe
                              so delicately

then smash it on the ground

in his native way
sucking out only the

                   easiest best red part.

So why does young Persephone who grew thirsty
have six seeds imbedded in her name
and how did the juice like wine
intoxicate her—so Hades could carry her off

Was *that* it—made the winter, made the anger
of her mother into winter

As she lay in a cavern with him
his tongue pushing at the
seeds still caught between her teeth

So little juice must have covered
those six seeds when sneaking
with no mirror she
broke her fast

Only enough to stain her teeth
when she smiled at him: *No. I've not
eaten anything.*

IV. ITALIAN HOURS

There you are at the origins of things
and your power to decide—paralyzed:
a bit later you'll leave,
to reassume a face.
                    —*Eugenio Montale*

CONFESSION

Yesterday—quickly—I had
three lovers—or rather
allowed myself to enter
be ravished
by three who touched
every part of me:
First, quickly, Monterosso—who was
hot for me midday after a climb
through bamboo and olives and a taste
of wild berries on the hillside.
Next a little beach—whose name
I can't remember—at Portofino
after the lighthouse nodded in
the afternoon sun.
Then, most dangerous—
whipping my hair back in ecstatic
sweepings of *tramonto*
light—while schools of feeding fish
were knocked into and out of
an aquamarine pool—
there, I gave myself (as the mussels
relaxed their doors)
even my fear—which is
the only kind of giving the sea
can know or profit from—
there, to Vernazza, with the washed
butternut campanile chiming the hour
of *ciao* to the sun before the fishermen
would descend, an hour or two later,
with their phosphorescent lures
to keep them wedded to the shore
or else they, too,
would have plunged
into the dark blue pool where all
desires whirl and start.

PORTOVENERE

Even here—wanting to enter *into* things
not circle round them
to draw close to a flame but
without the sun-ache in between
the eyes.
Then a decision falters—
a boat is missed
then the round glare of cats' eyes
isn't enough—
nor is circling round
the three islands where I had thought
to purchase peace.

Only for minutes in between fear
and anxious breathing
in between two
cliffs of rock I swam—the water
buoying me over the reef of
coral and schools of feeding anchovies
electric blue fish the size of a word
the crackling of salt in my submerged ears
almost forgotten: shark-fear
the fear of something, anything to hamper
in the delight of unknown lands.

Swimming in the *Grotta di Byron*
where he almost drowned on his way to Lerici
I did not drown.

MONTEROSSO-AL-MARE

Perfection rings out from these hills
terraced by time
and the sea, with its precise churnings

only I lack the perfection of being
just what I am
always this drive for more—this reach

though we pedal together on a boat, climb
the hill to where St. Francis is still feeding
the animals, guarding the small bay and town

I swim from the boat
always wanting more—
to be jostled into place

unnoticeable
among schools of feeding fish.
Perhaps that's what St. Francis wanted.

Even at sunset
when the tide should turn me inward
my ears still strain for

the music ringing in the stone steeple
that sings out, *I'm a stranger*
even to myself.

VERNAZZA

Green jade waters and eyes
the color of a young spring sky
and steps to make
our knees dizzy—grape-
vines terraced into the mountain view
and agave and bamboo.

We wound round the fishing boats
but could not wind round
each other—each tight-fisted
moment seething, bounded
by what we couldn't share.

Say it's not true.

The sea with its frisson of fish
swaying under the surface
of light-fissured
rocks.

What can I do to reach you.

The way the man carrying the basket
of covered grapes
seems indifferent
to the landscape
because he is wrapped inside it.

If only we could be wrapped
inside each other's story
maybe we, too, could
gather each other up—
with the same organic
indifference.

MANAROLA

Back in Monterosso
the parrot who never learned to sing
or fly sleeps in his wing,
having never found a better
use for it.

In Vernazza, the boys
still skid from the slippery rocks
into the crashing sea.

While here, in Manarola,
under a cloud, the sun
clefts to spray a flat circle
mid-sea, almost beyond our
ken—beyond any
sure swimmer's reach.
In this way
we pass into and out of
each other's care

        as the clouds
     hand the sun down
       to each
            other—a child's bright note
that the church steeple takes up.

PALIO

Siena

Once claimed from the sea
enter the frenzy
of drumbeats, banners

whipping
into the dry shell
of the Piazza del Campo

swept
and padded with sand
round its rim.

The wish to be a part
draws me
to the tops of towers

so the eye can embrace
horses, palaces,
rooftops of rose-tile

and remember
the stone lions inside the Duomo
still are giving suck.

TUSCAN LANDSCAPE WITH SELF-PORTRAIT

Arezzo

Bereft again
by the high wall
in the standing wind

his Sienese smile
red face
glistening body.

What did we see of San Gimignano:
the Piazza della Cisterna
(where we spilled into and over
each other)

towers where battles were tried
on pride,
how well the pulley of our bodies worked

there,
where we tried
to make a complete
forgetting of everything.

Now the purple wind soaks its way into
the cypresses,
now I count their peaks.

In Arezzo
as the German chorus chimes exaltations
to their god

I climb the path of olives
a dog warns of departures.

DIASPORA

The silent sunset falls on the mountains,
the children are out coursing the stone
steps of the town their grandparents built

And I, the Jew with light eyes, burn
in a solitude in the midst of their
joy and wonder:

Where are my people,
where is the path for avoiding
the spines that would prick my feet?

At two in the morning: a festival
of spaghetti, at two in the afternoon
a festival of tagliartelle with beans.

Here I sleep as though I have no need
of angels, and God talks directly
to me with no interpreter or intermediary.

MELANCHOLIA IN CASTIGLIONE
MESSER MARINO

In the light and air of who knows
what small village, with the after-
words of fire burnt in a copper
lid and watermelon after midnight

The thing to do is prepare
for lunch—roll out the tagliartelle
on a wooden board and cut them almost
as thick as a child's fingers.

Here the business is tomato sauce set by for the winter
boiled in huge vats outdoors
the smell of campfire everywhere
and wood stacked up against the wind
that first starts to blow
so sweetly, then rattles the clay shingles

                          from the roof.

Stones on the red tiles
to keep the wind from flying off
with them in winter.

The whine of the reservoir in the house
is a call to be careful
not to use too much of anything.

In the robust air—dogs, clogs on the pavements,
cat stealth, a woman's raised arms frozen

                          in a pose of dropping

dried favas from a basket, whose gypsy face asks,
Who are you?

PIAZZA DEI CAVALLI MARINI

Rome

Let the setter fetch the pine cone mid-fountain
let my toes drop into a cool pool to lure me
to stay and stay in the Villa Borghese and not go down
into the burning trafficked sea.

If this morning the ecstasy of Theresa
lasted only five minutes before the porter
began tamping out the candles and ordered,
All out, so be it; so did mine. Easier

To imagine the boy angel with his arrow flinched
withdrawing into a horny smirk—his wings, stone feathers—
as if he were about to re-attack—or pinch—
her in a swoon that had already transported her—forever

with stone-closed lids—as I, by these thrashing horses, homed
both legs into the cold sun of here, now, Rome.

OUT OF TIME

There the moon spilled its milk on the sea
the same that the sun in a torrent of clouds
had drenched in a circle far
out at sea.

In Orvieto
the church-face glittered
in the twilight as though it were
its own evening song.

The funicula filled up with its
hive of tourists
as we rolled down into
the consuming dark.

ROMA

In you, city of lions
from whose mouths
I've drunk
I've been ravished by time
passing its fragile cord between a long cool
morning and a lunch that unbeds me
into an evening on the Pincio
thick with sun and couples kissing.

Roma, you have made me sweat in the afternoons
and stripped me down to moist skin
at night.

You have shorn me of all wants
having lived a whole life in one month
ready to be retombed in the cold alabaster
of work, the metallic clang of the subway.

Nowhere—but here—is there such light
as in the Pantheon's solid rotating eye
or spilling from turtles
or pitchers poured by sea-gods.

Caravaggio's sad face, too, appears everywhere:
young David having slain his older self
hangs his heavy Goliathan head
from his youthful hand

As though it were possible to people the world with a single face.

Oh sick Bacchus, longing for
different fruit—a different
pair of lips.

LAST DAYS

are sweetest
the bells toll
the air of clear honey
filled with morning
voices, the Vespa's buzz

    from the terrace the wasps
    stop us from taking coffee outside.

Only remember: purple bougainvillea spilling
over railings
the scent of oleanders
opening their broad waxy petals
as though they were the palm of summer's
departing hand.

NOTES

Opening epigraph by Rilke translated by Stephen Mitchell.

"Praying Mantis in Brooklyn": The form of this poem, a sestina followed by a free-verse exposition, is modeled after Louis Zukofsky's "Mantis" and "Mantis, An Interpretation" (1934).

"Trivento": *Scamorsa* is smoked mozzarella; *dolce* are sweets; *temporale* is a storm.

"Canzone of Dreams": *Lusinghiero/lusinghiera* mean "enticing" or "alluring;" *lusinghieri* is the plural noun "enticements." Malatesta was an Italian Socialist. *Stanza* is Italian for "room."

"Thirst for More": *Contrade* are town districts in Siena, each named for an animal, which compete in the annual horse race called the Palio.

"Salvation": Epigraph translated by Rosemary Waldrop. *T'marim* are "dates."

"Spanish Snapshots": Some of the images in this poem were inspired by Henri Cartier-Bresson's photographs of Spain from the 1930s.

"The Colorblind Painter": For inspiration I drew on the artist's story told by Oliver Sacks in "The Case of the Colorblind Painter," which appears in *An Anthropologist on Mars*.

"ITALIAN HOURS": The epigraph is my translation of the final stanza of Eugenio Montale's poem "Portovenere," originally published in *Ossi di Seppi (Cuttlefish Bones)* 1925. This sequence is dedicated to the memory of Billy Gelfond.

"Confession": *Tramonto* is Italian for "sunset."

"Last Days": *Vespa*, an Italian brand of motor scooter, also means "wasp."